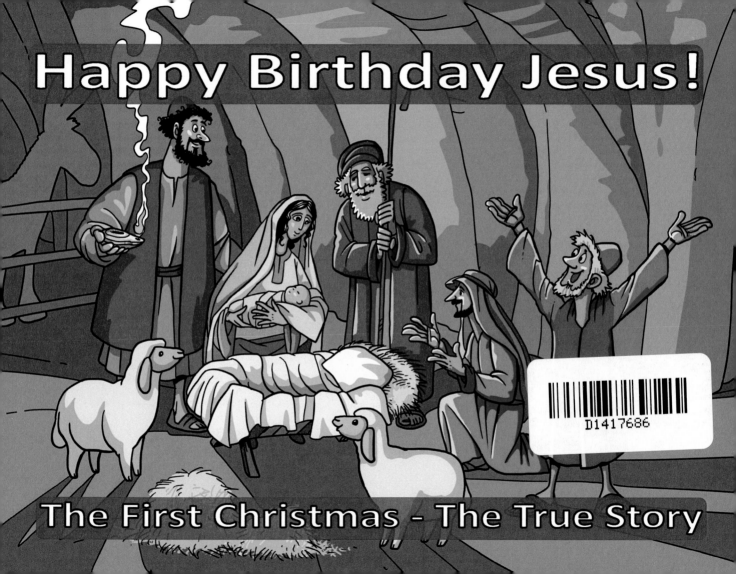

Happy Birthday Jesus!

The First Christmas - The True Story

It is with great appreciation that I feel the need to thank my husband Kent and son Brian for all their help. They sacrificed many hours of their time assisting me in many aspects of the writing and preparation of this book. I could not have done it without their help.

The author wishes to acknowledge the artistic contributions of the talented artist illustrators Askib, Dodrov Vitaliy, Vector-M and Mastapiece for the images used under license from Shutterstock.com

First Edition
Library Of Congress Cataloging In Publication Data on file.
ISBN: 9781520349442

Published in the U.S.A.

The story of the birthday of Jesus has been written down in the Bible for us in the books of Matthew and Luke. It's easy to see why God wants us to know about the birth of His Son Jesus and all the very special things that happened. The birth of Jesus is a wonderful and amazing story about two people. Their names were Mary and Joseph. God chose them to be the parents of His own Son. Jesus changed their lives and the lives of so many people around the world.

Many say that Christmas is the time for Santa Claus and for decorating trees and homes with lights. They say that Christmas is a time for lots of presents and parties. Too many people forget the true meaning of Christmas and why it is such a special time of year. The true story of Christmas IS about the birth of Jesus Christ. Christmas is so much more than crowded stores and getting presents and candy canes. It is the time of year to think about a very special baby that should have been born in a king's castle. Instead he was born in a barn where animals sleep.

About 2,000 years ago there was a woman named Mary and her husband named Joseph. They lived in a town called Nazareth by the Sea of Galilee.

God sent an angel named Gabriel to talk to Mary. When Mary saw the angel she was scared. Gabriel said to Mary, "Do not be afraid! Soon you will have a baby and you will name him Jesus" (which means savior). The angel told Mary that God was going to be the father of Jesus instead of her husband Joseph.

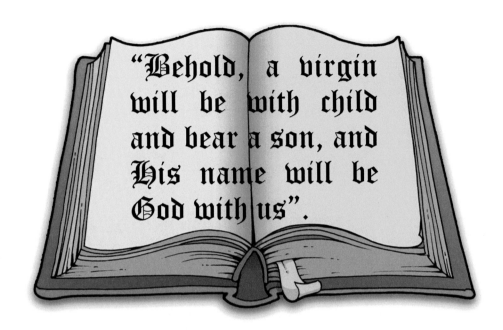

"Behold, a virgin will be with child and bear a son, and His name will be God with us".

Mary didn't understand how this was going to happen. But this is how God's Son was born into Mary and Joseph's family and came into the world as a man. The angel told Mary, "Jesus will be a great person and God will make Him the King of all Kings." So Mary believed the angel and said, "Okay!".

Just before Jesus was born a King named Caesar Augustus decided to count all the people in his kingdom. The King sent out a message to everyone ordering them to go back to the city where their family was from.

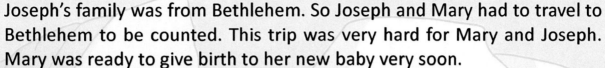

Joseph's family was from Bethlehem. So Joseph and Mary had to travel to Bethlehem to be counted. This trip was very hard for Mary and Joseph. Mary was ready to give birth to her new baby very soon.

There were no cars back then. People walked everywhere they went or they rode on camels or donkeys. It took Mary and Joseph about seven days to get to Bethlehem. They needed to travel slowly.

Fathers and mothers worked hard to take care of their families. Some people were farmers. Some were shepherds. Some were carpenters who made things with wood and stone. Joseph was a carpenter. All the work that each family did had to stop until they came home from this trip. This must have cost those families a lot of time and money! But everyone had to obey the Kings Decree.

When they finally arrived in Bethlehem Joseph wanted to keep Mary safe and warm. They planned on staying at the inn which was like a hotel.

But when they got there the innkeeper said, "Sorry! There's no more room! You will have to find somewhere else to stay!"

The only place Joseph could find that was warm and dry was a stable where farm animals sleep. It was the best he could do that night.

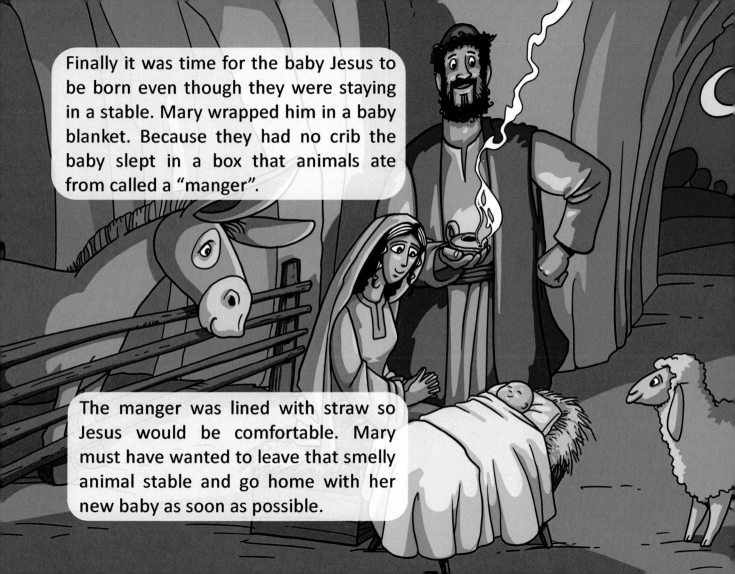

Finally it was time for the baby Jesus to be born even though they were staying in a stable. Mary wrapped him in a baby blanket. Because they had no crib the baby slept in a box that animals ate from called a "manger".

The manger was lined with straw so Jesus would be comfortable. Mary must have wanted to leave that smelly animal stable and go home with her new baby as soon as possible.

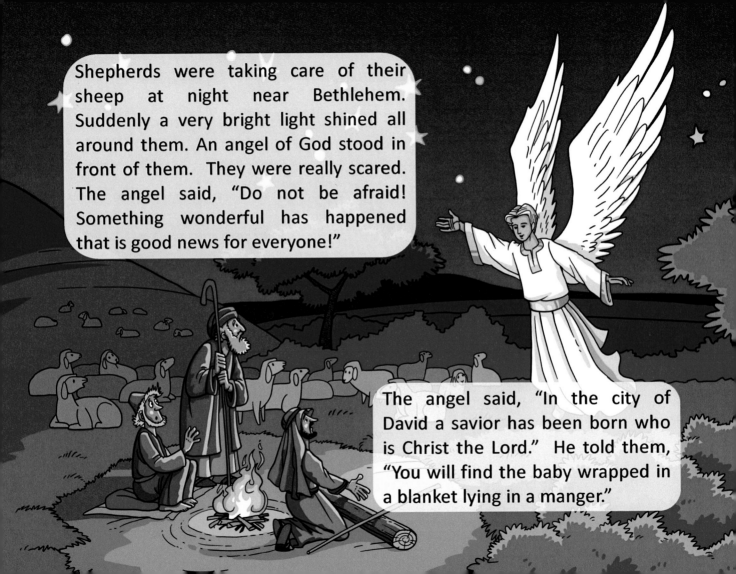

After that many other angels joined the first angel saying *"Glory to God in the highest and on earth peace among men with whom God is pleased."* Then the angels went back to heaven. What an amazing thing to see!

Mary and Joseph and the new baby Jesus were also visited by the Magi. Magi were known as Magicians or Astrologers. The Magi saw a special star in the sky that guided them. They wanted to find and worship the one who is called *"King of the Jews"*.

There was a bad King in Jerusalem named Herod. He became jealous when he heard about the birth of the new king Jesus. King Herod asked the Magi to find Jesus. He lied and said he wanted to worship Jesus. But he really wanted to hurt the baby Jesus.

The Magi went to find Jesus. The star they saw in the sky led them. The star stopped over the place where Jesus and his parents were staying. How great is that? And without any maps or G.P.S.!

When the Magi found Jesus they fell down and worshipped Him. They gave Him wonderful gifts of gold, spices and perfume. God warned the Magi not to go back and tell King Herod where Jesus was. So they went home a different way.

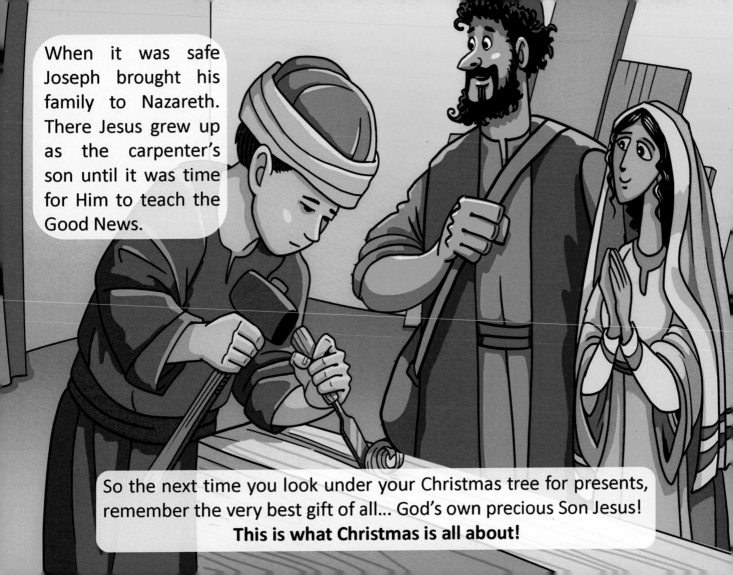

This book is dedicated to my four most precious gifts, my grandchildren, Jacob, Julia, Luke and London. My hope and prayer is that they, along with all the other children who read this small book, never forget what we should be remembering during the holiday season… That God sent His unique and special Son into the world to save us.

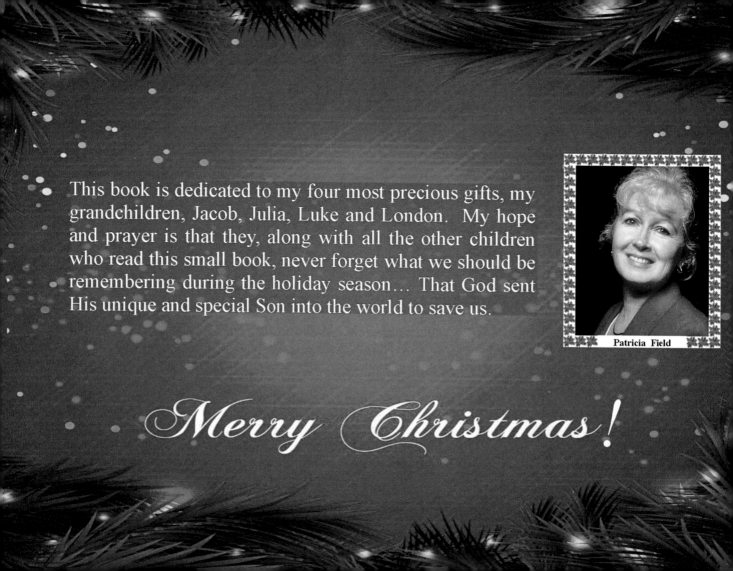

Patricia Field

Merry Christmas!